Conversations Between Me and The Kid.

Conversations Between Me and The Kid.

*Learning to parent through
conversations with my toddler.*

Phnewfula Y. Frederiksen

Turtle Pie LLC
  159 N Marion Ave, Ste
343
  Oak Park, IL 60301
www.shophappymang
o.com
Phone: 1-888-254-0611

Forward

All of my life I've lived in my self-centered Leo universe.
I have done as I pleased for the better part of 30 years.
I've worked very hard and followed my passions. I have
always done whatever I pleased. As the oldest of 3
girls I always knew I had a maternal instinct but I never
thought about using it. Especially, not at the time of
fertilization.

At the age of 29 I was in a whirlwind romance with
the kid's dad. He was out of town on my birthday
and when he came back boy did I get one hell of a
birthday present. By late September I realized I was
pregnant. That still remains one of the best birthday gifts
ever!

There is nothing that could have prepared me for this
little delicious ball of chocolate that is our son. He looks
just like his father and acts just like me. As he began
to grow and express himself I realized I had a mini me
on my hand. At the age of 35 I still have the sense of
humor of a 15 year old suburban boy. The kid is not too
far behind. My job requires consistent travel and when
it allows I take him on the road with me. The kid has
been exposed to so much at such a young age that
some of the conversations we have are well beyond his
years. I mean how many 3 year olds will specifically ask
for shrimp pad Thai and mango sticky rice for dinner.

I started keeping track of the conversations when the
kid was about 2 ½ years old. I began to realize some
of the stuff that came out of his mouth was just plain
funny. I think what made it even funnier to me is that
he speaks just like me! It is not unusual to hear him say
to one of his friends "dude, stop that!" Or if he drops
something he'll shout "darn it" or "sugarbooger" all

phrases I use quite often. Or when asked what he would like for breakfast saying "I actually think I'd prefer cereal please mom" is a normal answer for him. I thought to myself, I must write these down.

As he got older the conversations became more complex and at times more ridiculous than I could possibly even imagine. At three they were really, really, funny as he tried to express himself with words he didn't quite know yet or misidentifying things. At four I could not believe I was talking to a four year old. I am certain I was talking to myself or at least a teenage boy version of myself. This was further confirmation for me that this needed to be documented.

I began to post our conversations on facebook just so I wouldn't be the only one privy to the kid's banter. A few of my friends encouraged me to document our conversations, get a TV show or write a book. This is me killing two birds with one stone and maybe the TV show on the Travel channel will come☺

I have never been the mother who thinks that her kid is more special, funnier, or smarter than any other kid; I do at this point while I only have one, think he is the overall most spectacular boy in the universe. I do know that as a mom we can all relate and laugh at the things our children say.

I dedicate this book to all the moms who love to laugh at and with their children.

To the muses Agya, Maya, Joi, and De La, I'm sure you will continue to amuse for years to come.

Conversations between me and the kid

Conversations about us/family

January 24th 2011
M: Go put your bat in your room.
TK: No thank u.
M: That wasn't a question.
TK: Don't worry I don't have to put it back (hugs me) it's ok mom.

January 30th 2011
The kid is watching backyardigans and when the music comes on I started dancing.
TK: *yelling* Mom, stop dancing and go clean the kitchen!
M: I can dance if I want to.
TK: Mom you have to clean the kitchen.

July 1st 2011
TK: Mommy you are not waking up
M: Stop whining I am up
TK: No mommy, you are not up. You have to put your toes on the floor

November 10th 2011
Conversation between me and the kid after his dad calls to talk to him and he accidentally hangs up.
TK: Daddy, daddy hello?
Me: What happened to your dad?
TK: I don't know maybe . . . . he went to Africa?

December 23rd 2011
Conversation between me and the kid after I picked
him up and gave him a big hug.
TK: Mom put me down
M: I said but I loooooooove you!
TK: I love you too mom but you have to put me down,
I'm too big

March 22nd 2012
M: Ohayo gozaimasu
TK: Ohayo gozaimasu cutie pie!
M: Cutie pie? Where did you learn
that?
TK: From Africa.
M: Africa?
TK: Yea mommy, at the market and the other little boys
say that mommy.
M: . . . .

June 22nd 2012
TK: Mom did you download angry birds, the new one?
M: Oh, I'm sorry baby I did not.
TK: Because you don't have an iPhone?

July 11th 2012
Conversation between me and the kid after I told him
we were going to Toronto to see his cousin.
TK: Mom, how can I talk to him? Does he speak English?
M: Yes, he speaks English?
TK: So do I say bonjour to him?
M: No that is French
TK: See mom it's too much I told you I don't know how
to speak English

July 27th 2012
TK: Mom can I go to Alexis' house
M: Who is Alexis?
TK: She goes to my school

M: Oh, baby I don't know Alexis so you can't go to her house

TK: MOMMY, she's a girl like you. She has fluffy hair and legs.

Good to know if the kid had to describe me I'm fluffy hair and legs

August 18th 2012

M: Agya please don't do that

TK: MOM, you're talking too much and its making my ears hurt

M: Excuse Me????

TK: Yes, mom when you talk too much I don't like it. My ears will get blood.

August 20th 2012

Conversation between me, the kid, and my mom.

MM: Phnewfula stop it

TK: No, she doesn't have to stop. My mom can do whatever she wants!

MM: No she has to listen to me, I am her mother. You listen to your mom don't you?

TK: Yes, I listen to my mommy all the time, don't I mommy?

M: Yes, baby you do

MM: See she has to listen to me or I will whip her butt

TK: Nanaa (my mother) you are not allow to whip people's butts. That is not nice. My mommy is the boss and she can do all kind of things. She doesn't have to listen to you.

September 1st 2012

M: Hold my hand please

TK: No mommy ninjas don't need to hold their mommy's hands

M: What?

TK: I'm a ninja mom. You have to call me ninja

M: Well ninjas who don't hold their moms hand get time
out
TK: geez maneez mom

September 17th 2012
TK: Mom, can I have the GPs?
M: Why? Where are you
going? TK: To St. Louis
M: Oh wow, what's in St.
Louis?
TK: A talent show!
M: Well what are you going to do for talent?
TK: I'm going to show the iPad

September 19th 2012
Conversation between me and the kid after a big
meal. He grabs my stomach and . . .
TK: Mommy, who is in there?
M: There is no one in there
TK: Is there a baby in there?
M: No there is no baby in there!
TK: Well who's in there mommy? Tell me who!
M: There is no one in there dude
TK: I want a baby in there
M: Go talk to your dad
TK: Daddy how do we get a baby in mommy's belly
D: WhaaaaaaaaaaaaaaaaaaaaT????? Ask your mom
TK: Mommy, how do we get a baby in there
M: Daddy has to put on in there
TK: Daddy can we have a baby in mommy's tummy?

November 19th 2012
Conversation between the kid and my mom after she
told me to be quiet.
TK: You don't say that to my mom. That is not nice. You
need to be respectful. I don't like it when you say that
MM: I can say whatever I want to her
TK: Don't be disrespectful to my mom; she can do
whatever she wants. She's cute, and she cooks me all

kind of things to eat. She's nice to you; she does nice things for you all of the times. You have to 'pologize
MM: ok

November 21st 2012
TK: Mommy did you know poopoers (my sister) took your shirt home. She was wearing it.
M: Yes, I know she forgot her pjs
TK: Well I don't want you to share with her
M: We are supposed to share with our family. She is my sister.
TK: Your sister? When you were a little girl?
M: Well, yes.
TK: And was daddy a little boy?
M: Yes, he was.
TK: And I was a baby?
M: No you weren't here yet.
TK: Because it wasn't my birthday party yet?

November 23rd 2012
Conversation between me and the kid while watching the movie Jump the broom
TK: Mommy are they getting married?
M: Yes they are
Tk: Why are they getting married?
M: When two people love each other they get married.
TK: Are we married to each other?
M: No baby, we can't be married you're my son
TK: But I love you!!!
M: I know babe, but you have to marry another girl
TK: Is she going to have a son?
M: No you can have one after you get married
TK: Can I call him simba?
M: You can call him whatever you want

December 1st 2012
Conversation between me & the kid after I came in from being out.

TK: Mom where have you been? I was worried about you!
M: I had to go out to an event. I'm fine no need to worry.
TK: You can't go out because I love you. You were gone for 5 minutes
M: Well it was a bit longer than 5 minutes but I'm back now
TK: Why did you take so long?
M: Because that's how long my meeting was
TK: You can't just go out talking to people for a long time mom. I love you so you just can't do that
M: Kk, sorry:-(

January 26th 2013
Conversation between me, the kid, and the cashier at home goods.
TK: Hey, you don't talk good
TC: Well I can't tell you why that is. *Laughing* (former smoker)
TK: Mommy, that lady doesn't talk good. She talks like this (imitating her deep voice). She talks like a daddy.
M: Her voice is just different, that's ok
TK: No mommy I don't like that kind of voice.

February 12th 2013
M: Do you know how these teeth marks got on my blinds
TK: No. I didn't do it
M: The only other people who have teeth in the house are me and your dad and we didn't do it
TK: Did Sydney do it? No. Did Kingston do it? No. did Agya do it? No. I don't know who did it mom.
M: You don't know who did it?
TK: I did it. No! I didn't do it! hmmmmmmmmmmmmmm (with finger on chin)
M: Agya, did you bite my blinds?

TK: No, those look like baby teeth. These (pointing to his mouth) are big teeth for biting big things. I just don't know who did it mom.
M: Go to your room
TK: Are you mad at me?
M: Go to your room.

March 4ᵗʰ 2013
Conversation between me & the kid while he's in the bathtub.
M: Do you want to stay in here while I do my report?
TK: No your report needs to die and just get me out of the bathtub
M: My report cannot die, I need to do it so I have some money
TK: You don't need money, you need to get your kid out of the bathtub
M: If we don't have money we can't have a birthday party
TK: Mom, it takes a lot of work to do what you do mom. It takes a lot of work

Conversations about school and learning

August 15ᵗʰ 2011
My twitter alert is a bird chirp.
TK: Mom what's that noise?
M: Twitter.
TK: Twitter? What's that twitter? I don't like that twitter mom

Jan 19ᵗʰ 2012
Conversation between me, the kid, and his teacher.
TK: I need chopsticks
T: Chopsticks are only for lunchtime

M: Baby, you don't need chopsticks for your lunch today
TK: I do, I need chopsticks mommy
M: Ok, later at lunch
TK: MY lips are dry!! I need my chopsticks now!

Jan 20th 2012
M: Hi baby did you have fun at school today?
TK: School is not for fun, it's for learning
M: Ok, what did you learn in school today?
TK: I didn't learn anything I was not listening.
M: Why weren't you listening?
TK: Because I didn't do it, because I didn't listen,
because I don't want to.

May 7th 2012
TK: Mommy, it makes me sad when you don't know
your numbers and colors
M: But I know my numbers and colors?
TK: Well tell me what color is the stop sign
M: It's red
TK: Tell me the truth mom.
M: I am its red!
TK: No, you are not telling the truth it's an octmagon
(octagon)
M: That is the shape not color.
TK: Ohhhhhhhhhhhhhhhhhhhhhhhhhhhhhhhhhhhh shape.

January 14th 2013
Conversation between me, the kid and his classmate
TK: Mommy!!! I missed you today.
M: I missed you too did you behave today?
TK: Yes, I behaved myself allll day!
CM: Well, he didn't behave himself during reading time.
He was talking
TK: (putting his hand up to block her from talking)
Caroline, I can handle this myself.

March 8th 2013
M: Please get dressed so we can go to the library
TK: I don't want to go. I'm going to stay here by myself
M: You cannot stay home by yourself
TK: My teddy bear will watch me. No parents just me and my teddy bear
M: I'm going to go with no on that one. Get dressed
TK: It's my future mom and I can do what I want. I just want to stay home and be alone with myself
M: When I'm done, if you are not dressed we are going to have a problem.

Conversations about bed, potty and animals

March 14th 2011
I was reading the kid a bedtime story and it showed a cow making milk.
TK: Ewwwwwww mom the cow is pooping
M: No, it's making milk.
TK: No mom, that's not milk, he's pooping and it's yucky! Milk comes from the refrigerator

April 8th 2011
TK: Mommy, can you draw me an elephant?
M: Sure *draws elephant*
TK: That is not an elephant!!!!!!!!!!!!!

August 24th 2011
Last night the kid comes in my room around 2am
TK: Mommy can I get in your bed?
M: No, to go back to your bed.
TK: *yelling* MOM you are not being nice, you are not sharing!!

Jan 4th 2012
It's 9:46 and the kid is still coming in the living room every 15 minutes.
TK: Can I give you a hug?
M:* ignore*
TK: Can I give you a kiss?
M: *ignore*
TK: Can I give you a hi five?
M: *ignore*
TK: Oh mom can I have onigiri for lunch tomorrow?
M: *ignore*
TK: Mom I just want to dance one time before I go to sleep.
M: *ignore*
TK: Mom, how about I just sleep on the couch next to you?
M: You have 2 seconds before I close your door!

June 8th 2012
TK: Mom, are you going to take a nap with me?
M: No, I am working.
TK: When you finish working?
M: No, I won't be finished working.
TK: But mom, you need to rest, how you don't have any rest mom?
M: Because I'm working!!
TK: Mom, I will wait for you so we can nap together ok?
M: GO TO sleep!!!!!!!!!!!!!!

August 25th 2012
TK: Mom, I can't go to sleep there is a bee in my room

M: No there is not. Go to sleep
TK: I can't mom the bee will get
me
M: The bee will fly out of your room
TK: No it won't mom
M: Ok, show me the bee *walks into the room* show me
the bee
TK: Well when I was watching iron man I saw the bee
mommy
M: *cutting him off immediately* GO TO Bed!

December 17th 2012
M: Get back in the bathtub!
TK: Or I can't watch max & ruby?
M: You cannot watch max & ruby because I don't like
your attitude
TK: Mom, I talked to my attitude and it's not listening. I
said "you have to behave" and it's not listening.

Conversations about manners and Discipline

August 18th 2011
TK: Mom what's that?
M: It's a pimple.
TK: Mom, the pimple hurt you?
M: Yes:-(
TK: Well I have to call the police and tell them the
pimple is not being nice!

November 4th 2011
M: You must be really tired because you are
misbehaving
TK: No I'm not tired; I'm misbehaving because I love
you. I'm a good boy. If you want me to stop you just

have to say "agya stop it please" but I'm not going to go to my room. Ok mom?

March 31st 2012
Conversation between me, the not old at all nurse, and the kid.
TK: Mom, that old lady is trying to talk to me
M: Who?
TK: That old lady right there
The nurse: Who me?
TK: Yes You! You are trying to talk to me
M: Agya, it's not nice to call people old lady
The nurse: Oh my God I am not old!!
TK: She is an old lady mom.
The nurse: I'm only 32. I can't believe he just called me an old lady. I am not old!
M: He is 3 anyone over the age of 7 is old.

April 20th 2012
Conversation between me and the kid after I tapped him on the butt w/my foot to get his attention.
TK: Mommy your feet are not for touching people in the bum. They are for the ground.
M: I apologize, you are right. I was just trying to get your attention.
TK: Then you should say "agya will you pay attention please and I will say yes, of course I will pay attention mommy"
M: Ok it won't happen again

September 28th 2012
Conversation between me and the kid after I squeezed his hand for misbehaving
TK: MOMMY!! Why did you squeeze hand???
M: You weren't listening
TK: You don't squeeze my hand you only squeeze lemons and oranges
M: If you don't listen I will absolutely squeeze your hand

TK: No you do not squeeze my hand! I am not orange juice!!!!

December 8th 2012
Conversation between me and the kid after he brings me a handful of needles
M: Are these from the Christmas tree??
TK: Yes, because I shaked it
M: Do not shake the Christmas tree
TK: Too late I did already
M: Watch yourself, and do not touch the tree
TK: Why did you put it by me if you don't want me to touch it then?
M: GO TO YOUR ROOM!!

December 22nd 2012
TK: Mom I really love being with you.
M: I love being with you too but it hurts my feelings when you don't listen.
TK: MOM! We are not talking about that!

Conversations about fun

November 19th 2011
TK: Mom, can I ride the elephants?
M: No
TK: Mom what do you call the people up there?
M: Acrobats
TK: Oh mommy can I get up
there?
M: No
TK: Well what can I do then mom? What can I
do?
 M: Just watch the show

December 2nd 2011
Conversation between the kid and Santa at the mall
Tk: Hi Santa!!! Do you have my presents?
S: Oh, I will bring them on Christmas.
TK: Oh? Well where are your
reindeer.
S: At the zoo
TK: Oh? Well I want a rocket ship. Can I have it
now please?

December 23rd 2011
Conversation between the kid and one of my hip hop
artist.
A: Hey lil' man what's your name?
TK: Agya
A: How you feelin' you chillin'?
TK: No, I'm agya
A: I know, are you chillin'?
TK: No I'm a-Jah!!!!!!

Jan 23rd 2012
TK: Mom are we going to the gym?
M: No, we don't go to the gym anymore
TK: Why mommy?
Me: Because I was paying money for something we
don't use
TK: Well mommy you need to get some money to pay
for it so I can go play.

April 24th 2012
TK: Mom I want to take my he-man DVD
M: No, I don't like that one it has too much fighting
TK: Yes, and shooting, and monsters, and bad guys
M: Yes, I don't like for you to watch that kind of stuff
TK: Well then don't buy it. If you don't want me to
watch it just don't buy it mom.

May 16th 2012
Conversation between me and the kid, while he's
watching Celts vs. 76ers
M: Who's winning?
TK: The brown one
M: What brown one there is only green and white
TK: No, the brown one is winning mommy
M: There is no brown? What are you talking about show
me?
TK: That one mommy, the brown man is winning

July 15th 2012

Conversation between me and the kid after noticing a fair across from our hotel.

TK: Mom!!!!!! Can we go there?

M: I don't know do you know how to behave?

TK: Yes mom! I know how to behave; I am behaving all the days' mom! I know all the rules. I know how to listen. I know all kinds of things.

M: Ok we'll see

TK: MOM, I just Told you. I know, now let's go!

February 18th 2013
M: Mommy is going to the movies
TK: To see what mommy? What are you going to watch?
M: Lincoln
TK: Ohhh can I go?
M: No, I don't think you will like it
TK: I will like it! I love Lincoln! He's my favorite
M: Laughing, you don't even know who that is
TK: Yes mom! I love him. It's the best movie in the history (of movies)
M: *laughing*, dude, you can't go. Mommy needs just a little quiet time
TK: Fine! But I don't like it when you go someplace without me.

Conversations about food and clothes

Jan 7th 2012
M: Baby, go get your slippers
TK: MOMMY, I don't see them. I looked up high, I looked down low. Maybe . . . . they just madeappeared (disappeared).

Jan 25th 2012
So the kid hands me a bag a mangos to open and I can't get it open without scissors.
TK: Mom, you can do it
M: Baby I can't do it without scissors
TK: You can do it mommy just keep trying
TK: *I finally get the bag open he pats me on the head* oh mommy I knew you could do it

March 29th 2012
M: Do you want mushrooms on your pizza?
TK: No, I don't like mushrooms.

M: yes you do.
TK: no because my daddy said mushrooms are only for girls so that's why I can't have any.

July 12th 2012
Conversation between me and the kid. Ruth Chris style
M: do I need to order the chocolate molten cake in advance?
The waiter: no m'aam you do not
TK: Oh mom I don't want to eat food just dessert
M: No you have to eat dinner first
TK: Remember mom I ate already this morning.
M: Yes, but you have to eat dinner. You need to eat 3 times a day
TK: 3 times????? Oh mommy that is a lot of times

July 24th 2012
TK: Mom, you don't have any pants on
M: I know, I have on a dress
TK: You need to put pants on like me
M: No, girls don't wear pants with dresses
TK: Remember I looked under your dress and you said I was not supposed to do that?
M: Yes, you are not allowed to look under girls' dresses
TK: Fine, you can't come with me then if you don't want to wear pants. I don't like it when you don't wear pants. People will look under your dress.

August 9th 2012
M: Please go put your clothes on
TK: Ok
10 minutes later I discover he is still in his undies playing with his trucks
M: I thought I asked you to put your clothes on?
TK: Ohhhhhhhhhhhhhhhhhh that's what you wanted me to do. You don't want me to play with my trucks? Ok fine I won't play with my trucks.
M: Please hurry I have a conf call

TK: Can I watch TV during your conf call?
M: No get dressed
TK: Ok, ok you just have to be patient mommy remember.

August 22nd 2012
The kid and I have just come home and there is nothing but an echo in my fridge. The conversation goes like this:
TK: Mom can I have a granilla bar (granola bar)
M: No, are you hungry? If so I will take you to get something to eat.
TK: (2 minutes later) mom, can I have some yogurt?
M: No, go put your clothes on
TK: (still without clothes and 3 minutes later) mom, you don't have bananas or something?
M: GO get dressed and we can go get food
TK: (still with no clothes on and about 2 minutes later) mom, can I just have 3 (dried) cranberries in my hand please?

August 23rd 2012
Tk: Mom can I have macaroni and cheese?
M: No
TK: Why not mommy, I like it, it's tasty.
M: You have had macaroni and cheese 3 days in a row
TK: *yelling* MOM I deserve to have macaroni and cheese!

August 24th 2012
Conversation between the kid and oral hygienist
Oh: Do you know why we don't like gummy snacks?
TK: No, I like gummy snacks!
Oh: Well we don't like them because when you eat them you get cavities.
TK: No I don't. I don't have camaties I have clean teeth
Oh: *laughing*, well maybe in a few years you'll understand

October 19th 2012
M: Did you seriously just spill all of that milk????????
Tk: No mommy I didn't. It spilled itself. It wasn't my decision to spill it the milk.
M: :-/

November 17th 2012
TK: Mom, these clothes need to be washed because they are wet
M: How did they get wet?
TK: I found them in the toilet
M: And how did they get in the toilet?
TK: I threw them
M: Are you supposed to throw clothes in the toilet?
TK: No I didn't throw them they just got in there mommy, I just saw them
M: Agya . . . .
TK: I'm sorry mommy, I didn't do it on purpose, I know better. I'm going to go in my room so I can watch TV later after you think about it.

November 18th 2012
M: Mommy has to go to work later on ok?
TK: who's going to cook dinner for me?
M: Your dad
TK: no mommy, daddy doesn't know how to cook when you're gone. He just leaves me in front of the TV all the time. I'm gonna be hungry if you leave.
M: Ok, I will fix you something before I leave
TK: Thank you mom, you're the best ever!

March 4th 2013
TK: Mom is pork poisonous?
M: No! Who told you that?
TK: Nobody told me that. I'm just trying to figure out why we don't eat meat.
M: You eat meat. You just don't eat pork or beef. It's a personal choice.

TK: Some people eat pork?
M: Yes, some people do eat pork and that is fine.
TK: Are they bad guys?
M: No they are not bad guys.
TK: When I get bigger I can eat it?
M: If you so choose, yes you can.
TK: Thank you mommy you're the sweetest mommy ever.

Conversations about Travel

February 10th 2012
TK: Mom is it time to go on the airplane?
M: Yes, are you going to sleep?
TK: No I'm just going to sit up.
M: Why aren't you going to sleep?
TK: I just want to talk mom.

July 23rd 2012
M: Baby we are going to San Diego!
Tk: Are we going to see Dora?
M: No? We are going to see Shamu.
TK: Why are we not going to see Dora?
M: Dora is at the aquarium
TK: She is not with Diego?
M: Ohhhhhhhhhhhh no baby, San Diego is a place not a person. It's not Diego
TK: Dora is not going to be there?
M: No baby
TK: Because she is at the aquarium?
M: Yes.
TK: Is boots there?
M: Go get in the bathtub.

August 10th 2012
TK: Mommy you didn't pack my books?
M: If there are no books in your bag it's because you didn't pack them
TK: MOM I told YOU to pack my bag
M: No, you are responsible for packing your own bag
TK: (while shaking his head) mom I just don't know what I'm going to do with you.

August 22nd 2012
Conversation between the kid and the southwest airlines flight attendant
Tk: Can I have what's in your pocket please
FA: Sure, here are 3 bags for you (peanuts)
TK: Thank you very much but I want pretzels please
M: Baby, they only have peanuts
flight attendant swiftly disappears and reappears equally as quick
FA: Here you go! (turns to me) I heard him when he asked
TK: See mom, they always have what I want you just have to say please and they will give it to you. See mom, that's all you gotta do.

Random Situations

Things that happen in the bathroom

June 1st 2010
There is pee on the floor and only two people in the apartment. The kid says he didn't do and I'm know for damn sure I'm potty trained so who did it?

July 14th 2011
The kid was about to get in the tub when he asked me to get his new soap from the car. I told him to sit in the bathroom while I ran to the car. When I came back he was standing in our doorway butt naked yelling "mooom do you have my soap yet?"

October 30th 2011
I fell asleep on the couch last night and at about 2am I see the kid go by and make his way to my room. This morning he got up around 6:00am and came to get on the couch with me. At 5:20pm I finally go in my room and realize the kid has peed in my bed. I ask him about it and he says "oh yeah mom I peed in your bed sorry", "your bed is dirty now".

October 31st 2011
The kid is now playing spot the vagina. Since he now knows that women and men have different parts he wants to verify whenever possible. Tonight he asked me if one of his friend's moms had a nangina (vagina). I said "yes". Then my mother calls and he says "mom does nana (my mom) have a nangina?" I said "yes". he then comes into the bathroom and asks me if I'm going to use my nangina to pee.

November 17th 2011
This morning the kid wakes up while I was in the shower.
He asked if he could sit in the bathroom until I got out so I
said sure grab a magazine. He loves to read bon appétit
which I generally have in the bathroom. Apparently all
he saw was real simple and Instyle magazine so he says
"Mommy all these are only for girls!"

April 1st 2012
The kid and I were in my mom's room when her friends
came by. One of her friends has a 10yr old that the kid
used to play with all the time. The kid runs to give her a
hug then looks at her arm and says "you are browner
than me". I asked him where he learned that. He says
"from Africa mom" so her mom says "well is your mom is
brown too" he says "no silly my mommy is not brown".

July 20th 2012
I stuck the kid in the bathtub so I could finish cleaning
the kitchen. I heard him yelling for me and telling me
he was clean and I kept telling him 5 more minutes. By
the time I got in the bathroom I had a very angry kid
glaring at me. He said "mom, I'm not very happy at
you. You heard me calling you because I was clean
and I wanted to get out. I don't like it when you don't
come and get me. I am sleepy and you need to read
me a book so I can go to bed."

Random Situations—Bed

August 25th 2010
Nothing like finally getting home from work at
12:30am and as soon as I try to get in the bed I hear
"mooooooooom open door please" now he wants to
talk!

December 3rd 2010
The kid is supposed to be napping but instead he is
telling me how pizza wants to go to the party in his
tummy.

February 16th 2011
The kid has been asking me to get up for the last hour.
He just climbed in my bed snuggled next to my ear and
starts singing are you sleeping are you sleeping to the
tune of frère Jacques!

December 4th 2011
I just got off the phone with the kid's babysitter to see
how he slept. She informed me that he woke through
the night with several grievances. There were leaves in
his bed, his eyes hurt, there was a pencil in his eye, he
needed cookies, and lastly he couldn't sleep because
he needed to watch TV.

Jan 14th 2012
This morning when the kid woke up he came in my
room. he grabbed my phone off the night stand,
climbed in my bed, gave me a kiss on the forehead
and said "go back to sleep mom I'm just going to sit
next to you and play mad birds"

Random Situations—School and Learning

March 4th 2011
When I dropped the kid off at school this morning his
new teacher asked to speak with me. It wasn't a stern
asking so I figured it wasn't bad. The conversation went
like this:
Teacher: what language do you speak at home?
Me: we speak Japanese and English; I'm not fluent in
Japanese so it's about 30/70.

Teacher: Oh well that is probably the issue, we are having miscommunications. When I tell him to do something he does the opposite or he continues to do what it is that I told him not to do. I think he just doesn't understand what I'm telling him.

Me: Oh no, he understands English perfectly well; he is just not listening to you. He is just misbehaving.

Teacher: He's not bad. He behaves quite well other than that. The other teacher seems to understand him perfectly fine and he listens to her. (back story, the other teacher has been with him for the last year so he is familiar with her)

Me: He's just not listening to you. He misses his old teacher so he's trying to play tough so you send him back to his old class. You need to put him in time out if he continues that.

Teacher: No, no. There is no time out in my class. No discipline at all. I only ask that the kids listen. They can do whatever they want if they listen.

Me: Blank stare (thinking to myself "no time out?? Good luck with that lady! My kid is going to run all over you")

September 2nd 2011

I have now realized when the kid starts a sentence with "because, that's why" that is the equivalent to "well, what had happened was"

March 5th 2012

The kid is out of school today for teacher cleaning day so it's take the kid to work with you day! I am teaching him to say "please play my mommy's wale record so I can go to college", "if you put my mommy's Kirko Bangz record in power I can finally get that rocket ship that I always wanted", and last but not least "Jill Scott is a mommy, just like my mommy and if you don't play her record her son will be very, very, very, sad" Guess who's getting some records played today.

June 15th 2012
Today, I asked the kid how to spell my name and he says. 404—www-f as in frank-u-l-a. Apparently he has mixed in a webpage and my phone number with my name. At least I know he listens because when I spell my name for people I always say "f as in frank".

Random Situations—Food

March 9th 2011
Our waitress just told me the kid is such a blessing because he is so well behaved. I didn't want to end the kumbaya by telling her the only reason he's not throwing food is because he's tired!

March 19th 2011
At breakfast with the kid and he hands me his fork and says "here you go mom, I'm going to use my fingers" and now I have syrup in my hair . . . .

April 6th 2011
What would possess the kid to dip his wet wipes in my cup of tea???

July 8th 2011
Our very nice waitress asks the kid if she could take his plate and he yells "neveeeeeeeer" she said "ok well I'll let you continue to work on that".

July 23rd 2011
"Mom, I want to help you make pancakes with blueberries!"

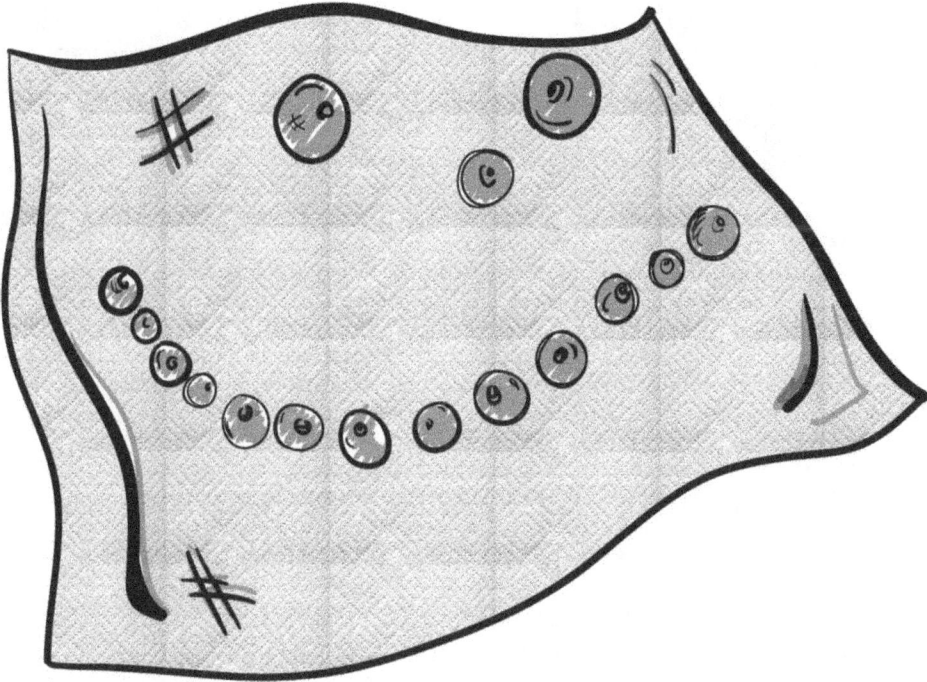

November 24th 2011
We went to breakfast this am and the kid had some
pancakes. The busboy picked up the kid's pancakes
before he was ready. When the waitress returned to
ask him how his pancakes were he said "that man took
my pancakes and I was not very happy" the very nice
waitress made the kid some new pancakes to take
home.

November 25th 2011
While I'm not paying attention and deciding between
hummus brands, the kid sticks his full face under a soda
fountain I didn't even see! All I hear is a running tap
and the kid saying "mmmm that's tasty".

Jan 1st 2012
He is still wide awake waiting for our midnight prayer.
he says "ohh mommy I don't feel good. My tummy
hurts I think I need a bagel with peanut butter".

Random Situations—Laundry & clothing

March 11th 2011
I ran out of the bathroom to grab the kid's pjs and
when I came back he had my bra in the sink "washing
it". Another case of monkey see monkey do gone
wrong!

July 6th 2011
The kid has better style than I do already at the age of
3. If I put a wife beater on him he yells "mom I need a
shirt!" he won't even wear one to bed. I clearly didn't
realize that wife beaters weren't real shirts until my early
twenties.

March 12ᵗʰ 2012
It's amazing how age and children bring a higher rise to your jeans. Before the kid I used to be the low rise jean queen I had Frankie B.'s in every cut, style, and color. Now I cringe when shopping for jeans and the tag says low rise. It took one time for the kid to say "mommy I see your bum" and it was a wrap for me!

April 23rd 2012
The kid picked out my shirt

Random Situations—Manners & Strangers

September 10th 2011
The kid was playing a video game on his dad's phone
and he says "shut up stupid" to the game. I told him
that wasn't very nice and we don't say words like that.
He says "ok I'm sorry mom I won't say it again but it's
not your problem".

November 2nd 2011
The kid and I are on the computer looking at pictures.
He gets up to put his cup away and says "mommy
don't move" when he comes back he says "you didn't
move mom, very good!" "You are a good boy mommy,
I love you very much"!

December 19th 2011
The kid and I are unsuccessfully working on him not
talking to strangers. After he gave a random lady on
the escalator a pound I told him again no talking to
people you don't know. He says "but mom I didn't talk
to her? I just did like this (showing his pound)" in the
next store a lady walks by and says excuse me the kid
yells "don't talk to us you don't know us!!!"

April 22nd 2012
The kid and I were in trader Joes and a lady was in
his way as he was trying to push his cart. He made his
way through so I asked him if he said "excuse me?"
Very matter of factly he says no I said "get out of my
way lady". I was absolutely mortified and I chased the
lady down to make him apologize. Thank God she
accepted his apology and said it was ok. I can already
feel 3 more gray hairs growing . . . .

Random Situations—Fun and Travel

November 23rd 2010
The kid has decided that he's a superhero. For the
past week or so every time he says he's a superhero
I ask him what superhero he is and he doesn't
have an answer. This morning when he told me
he was a superhero when I asked who he said the
gingerbread man. I told him the gingerbread man
wasn't a superhero and he yells "Yes I am gingerbread
superhero!" apparently the gingerbread man has been
upgraded to a superhero.

October 10th 2011
I was trying to occupy the kid while we were waiting for our food. He says "Mom can you draw me a pirate in a boat?"

April 25th 2012
The kid takes a 6:25am flight like a pro! Me on the other hand not so much. He was asking everyone in the business preferred lane where they were going and if they were getting on the plane with us.

May 15th 2012
Just a few things that I learned by having 3 toddlers in my house:
1. My bathroom door doesn't lock
2. What is a good idea for one is not necessarily good when multiplied by 3
3. One of the kids will inevitably want to eat off of the singular robot mat, causing a meltdown
4. The kid is not a very good host

Random Situations—family

December 5th 2011
My dad will be here tomorrow to take over duties with the kid. As I'm preparing notes for him and setting the menu, I'm dreading what kind of reaction I'm going to get when I tell him he has to cut the crust off of the kid's sandwiches for his lunch. I'm expecting a "get the hell outta here with that BS" or a "when I was growing up in st. Thomas we couldn't afford the bread. We ate butter and crust sandwiches dipped in beach water" type reaction.

December 8th 2011
The stories coming from my dad about the kid are sheer comedy! COMEDY!!! Between the two of them I don't know who's funnier. My dad gave the kid snickers and tells him not to tell me. He says "ohhhhh yes, thank you papa we can't tell mommy she will be angry at you". Like a good little boy he called to tell me anyway.

April 28th 2012
The day the kid met his cousin. He said "don't cry I love you"

May 11th 2012
This is the kid's portrait of me for mother's day! I would say he's spot on:-)
かわいい！

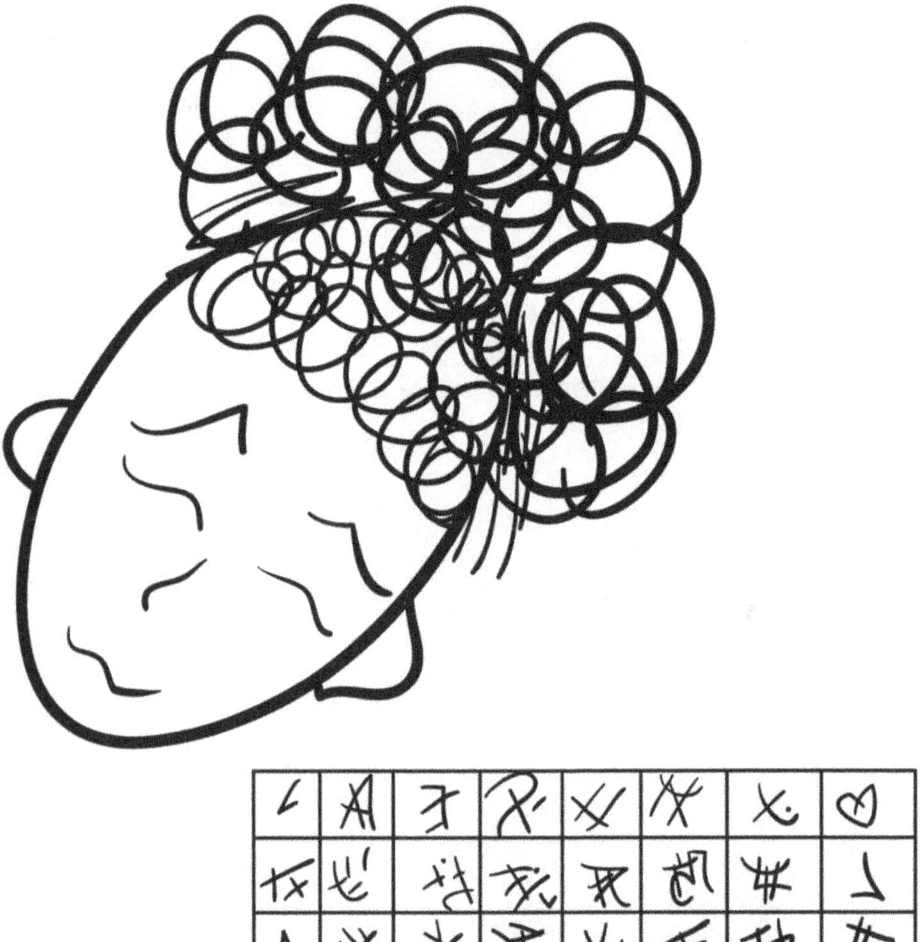

August 7th 2012
Now that my sister has had a child the kid always has random questions about childbirth and breastfeeding. Occasionally he will ask about how he was born and I tell him "you were in my stomach, I pushed really, really, hard and the doctor pulled you out" today when I told him he gave me an angry look and says "mom! The doctor is not supposed to pull people. He will hurt me and rip my shirt. I am not happy at him and I don't like it when he does that" instead of spending another hour explaining to him that he was born naked I just agreed and told him I would talk to the doctor about pulling.

September 13th 2012
We are redecorating and the kid's dad had some of his Kappa alpha Psi fraternity, incorporated. paraphernalia out to be put up. The kid found his dad's cane and from the kitchen I hear a big gasp and an "ohhhhhhhhh". He come running in the kitchen with his eyes wide and says "oh mommy how can we eat this big candy cane!!"

August 28th 2012
The kid's prayer for tonight.
God, can you please tell Santa to come to my House because I don't want him to forget. I know I'm supposed to be good but I didn't listen to my mommy in the store so can you make me good. I thank you for my life but I want Santa to bring me robots. Can I have a little sister? I want all the people to be happy when you build something for me. In Jesus name, amen.

October 22nd 2012
The kid's dad has connected his iPod to his iPad unbeknownst to me. I hear rap coming from the dining room and I walk in to find the kid listening to RIck Ross—God forgives I don't while doing his numbers.

March 5th 2013
Why is there a ninja turtle on my ceiling fan? According to my child "he was flying" I informed him turtles don't fly and he said "ok well maybe I threw it"

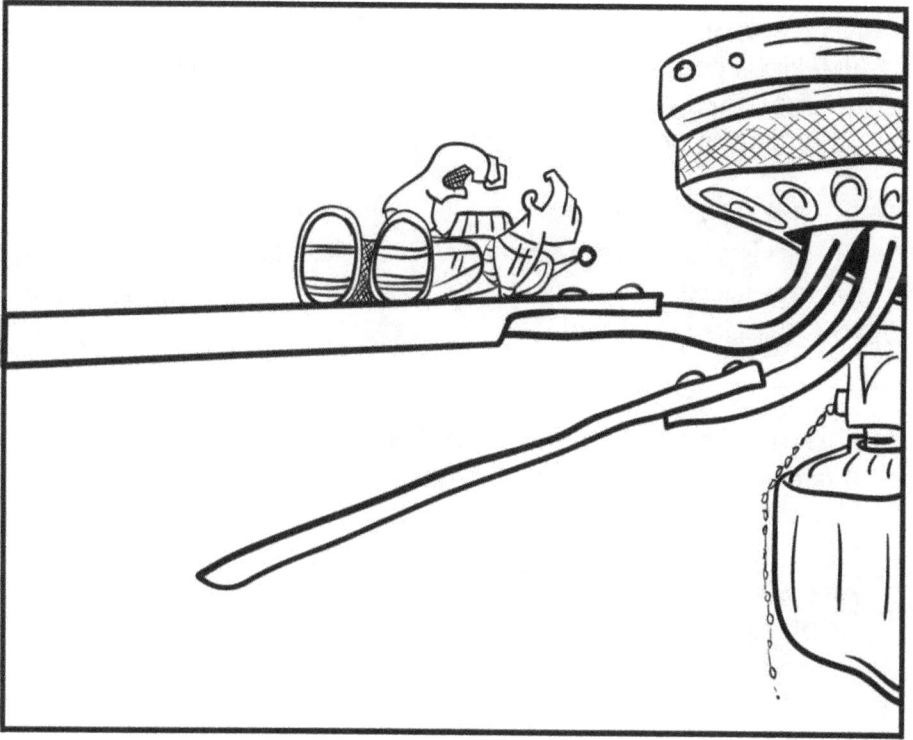

One Liners

The kid is the king of one liners. Like to hear em? Here they go!

November 10th 2010
The kid is playing with his electric car and when he realizes that it won't go he opens the battery door and says "mom we need some gas".

September 1st 2010
My kid is sitting next to me with a loaded diaper. He lifts his leg, looks down and says "eeewww mom you need to change pamper!"

December 12th 2012
I have on an E.T. shirt and the kid keeps yelling "mom there's a monster on your shirt!"

November 20th 2010
Are we having choco-lah-tay mom? (Chocolate chip cookies)

January 16th 2011
The kid and I were having pizza after church and he
says "I need to share my pizza with Jesus!"

May 19th 2011
The kid decided he wanted chipotle for his birthday
dinner. I asked if he wanted chicken or guacamole
and he said ummmmmmmm I think I'll have
wakamonie mom.

May 26th 2011
The kid walks up to the security guard in whole foods
and says "hey where's your fire truck?"

June 8th 2011
I made chicken fingers for dinner and when my mom
called and asked the kid what he was eating he said
"chicken hands!"

June 14th 2011
The kid got parakeets for his birthday and today I told
him they were pooping all over the place. He says
"because they don't have pull ups on mom".

July 2nd 2011
The kid is deliriously sleepy and he's trying to barter.
"Mommy I'm gonna go nite nite after you give me just
2 (dried) cranberries"

July 12th 2011
After being on the road for a few days the kid is
beginning to mock the GPs he just said "mom, are you
going to make slight right?"

July 21st 2011
I'm in the kitchen and the kid walks in to see me
dancing to Bell Biv Devoe's do me! He says "go mom

Shake your booty" I have the slightest idea where he got the word booty from.

August 6th 2011
The kid and I are about to go to the farmers market and the kid is riding his bike in the house. I told him to go put his bike in front of the door and finish getting dressed. He says "but mom there is no parking space".

August 11th 2011
I bent over to pick up a bag and apparently my underwear was showing so the kid says "mom do you have on pull ups?"

September 26th 2011
"Mom I parked all of my cars so they can go to sleep"

November 9th 2011
The very nice man at the Honda dealership shows the kid a picture of his family and the kid says "I don't like your family, they are not dressed up".

November 12th 2011
The kid and I were out for breakfast and I asked him what kind of pancakes he wanted he says "I want pancakes that are brown like me. I am brown. You are yellow like eggs mom".

November 27th 2011
"Mom, can I have a bath bomb in my bath?" I am sure I have the only 3 yr old in America who request a bath bomb instead of bubbles.

March 20th
"Mommy you cannot see me because I'm hiding"

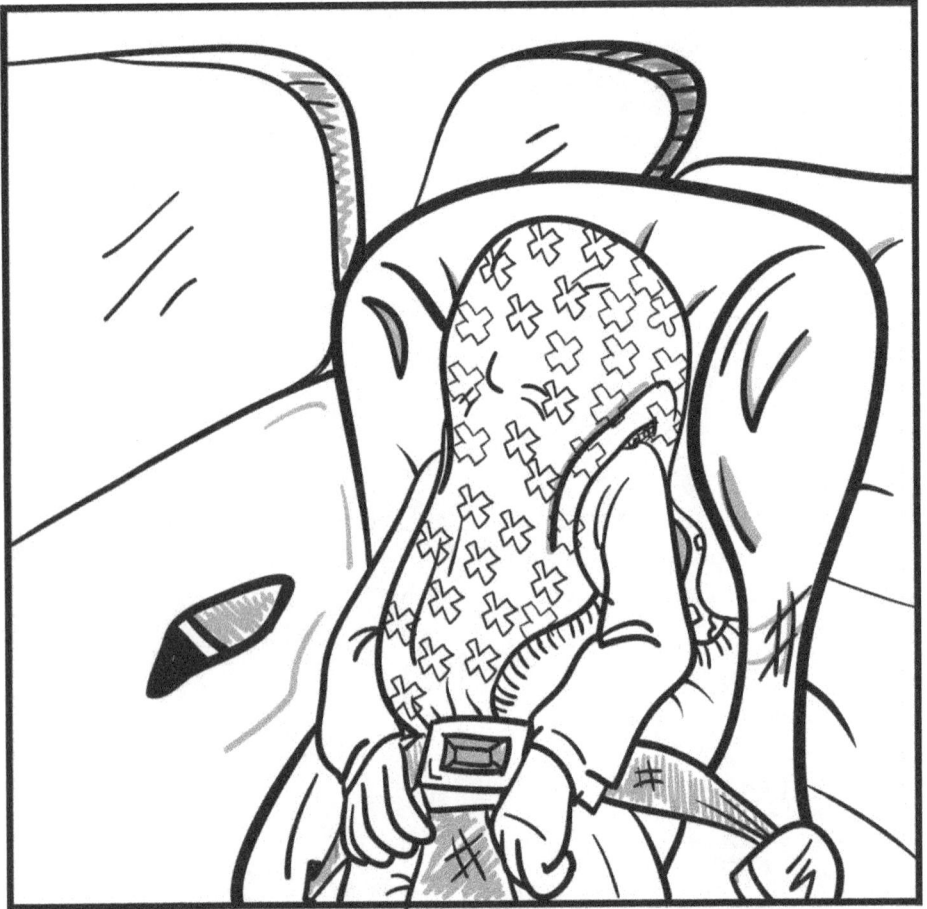

March 22nd 2012
The kid and I just sat down to enjoy our chipotle dinner and he's very angry he looks at me and says "mom there is no yogurt on my taco!" By yogurt he of course means sour cream.

May 27th 2012
I called the kid to tell him I'm at the airport and I'm on my way home and he says "ok mom but you have to take a taxi because we are not coming to get you".

June 5th 2012
I was just explaining to the kid that I am leaving tomorrow. He says "mom, you cannot go for a long time because I worry about you and I miss you when you're gone".

September 11th 2012
"Mom, I just want you to call me the masked retriever from now on".For the rest of the day he would answer to nothing else but.